Elements & Angels

Poems
by

Apryl Skies

Edgar & Lenore's Publishing House Tucson AZ 85705
eapeditors@gmail.com

Editing - Apryl Skies Foreword - Rick Lupert
Photos – Apryl Skies, Alexis Rhone Fancher
Cover – Apryl Skies, Eric Lawson

ISBN: 978-0-9987118-1-2
Imprint: Edgar & Lenore's Publishing House

Printed in the United States Of America
First Edition 2026

Elements
&
Angels

poems

by
Apryl Skies

DISCLAIMER:

This book is written with tragic optimism and equally hopeful pessimism.

TABLEAU

FOREWORD

Elements & Angels is a whole life told in poems — the bruises, the beauty, the weirdness, the grief, the humor, the ghosts, all of it. Apryl Skies writes in a voice that doesn't flinch. One moment she's admitting "a stone grows cold in my gut," and the next she's watching a "dragonfly find its place upon petals" while the world falls apart. That's the heartbeat of this book: the way devastation and wonder keep showing up in the same breath.

These poems wander through childhood, mothers, daughters, lovers, deserts, cities, and the strange aftershocks of memory. Skies digs up "little dead things," forgives what she can, buries what she can't, and keeps moving. Later the tone shifts — earthquakes, wildfires, "the sky a sackcloth of blackened tresses," the surreal chaos of daily life, the tenderness of old friends, the ache of what's gone, the humor of what's left. Even the haiku land with weight: a "Mai tai sunset sky," a city "buried beneath soot and ash," a plea to stay afloat.

Short pieces, long pieces, photographs — the book reads like a memory box cracked open. These poems don't just sit there; they shift, they breathe, they talk back. One even warns you, "This poem is subject to change without notice." These poems don't just break the fourth wall — they invite it in for coffee. Whether she's writing about Tom Petty, lizards on a hot rock, or the quiet burn of forgiveness, Skies brings a voice that's bold, intimate, and entirely her own.

This is a book about surviving yourself. About carrying what you can. About finding light in the wreckage. And somehow, Apryl Skies makes it feel like we're surviving together.

- Rick Lupert, Author of ***God Wrestler, a Poem for Every Torah Portion***; and proprietor at PoetrySuperHighway.com

A STONE GROWS COLD IN MY GUT

Because a child
is a tiny universe
wanting to believe
there is more to existence
than chance or circumstance

because a woman
was our first true residence
but now our lights
have dimmed and our homes
are no longer safe

A stone grows cold in my gut
because a man
can no longer fight with dignity
under the constant strain of injustice
when the only chance
of survival is survival itself

because humans
suffer in silence when greed
is the new universal currency
and because it is easier
to pivot our eyes and hearts away
than face our own shortfalls

A stone grows cold in my gut
because humanity
has more gravitas than fragile ego,
more depth than our dying oceans
and without humanity,
we dig our own shallow graves.

Have you ever seen a fairy ring?

HANDS

Our hands and their hold
first touch upon newborn skin
will heal or destroy

THE UNEXPECTED

Below a firelight, shining distance
Angels observe with wings spread wide
Orion arches his bow
Above the hills of Los Angeles
And beyond this hazy sky
Where an unexpected visitor
Enters Neptune's orbit,
Love spills over like wine or April rain.

In the air, a scent of something
Unexpected, destined, new.
Here an infant cries
In this crowded house
Where its weary eves bend
Beneath this heavy dale of time
And with the independence of St. Lucia
A ghost wanders these narrow hallways
Creaking the wooden floorboards
And tells a tale
Unfolding like a wailing accordion
In this settled unquiet.

An old woman rocks in her chair
With gray locks twisted tightly
Like a cinnamon pastry
Her tiny frame swallowed up
By colorful quilts sewn
With two crooked. calloused hands.

In the backyard orange groves bend
Bearing fruit, as the grapevine
Trolls the terrace in search of sun
And beneath this February tempest
Rabbits seek the dry warmth refuge
Of handmade hutches
Crafted with wire and wood

This day arrives with joy and fear
Tears of uncertainty and celebration
A bouquet of flowers
Stands tall in the dining room
And in its smiling, bold beauty

…renders the poet a name.

DOWNWARD DAUGHTER

Vivid memories scatter like starlings,
and I wish to undream the past,
repaint your melancholy into black lilies
on the grave of your suffering.

My earliest memory,
my infant self, held warmly
in the arms of my sister.
In my every dream of you

I wore that green checkered dress,
in my every recollection
your fractured sadness overcomes
like high tide, or sudden storm
crashing waves ebb and flow
into an unknown future.

Life as we know it,
a jigsaw puzzle of frayed ends
and unfinished memoir
the kind that never feels safe
an unending swallowing its own tail

I dream of your silence
and how you wore it proud
like a suit of armor.

In my every dream repeating,
unending as your silhouette fades
into the background of our muted sky
and your voice softens to a distant
echo of angels welcoming you
into a new and peculiar light.

little dead things

she came to me
with a quizzical grin
her hands so full of curious

a gathering of little dead things
locked in time-capsule gray
she stared back in a faint whisper

why?...

because nothing lasts forever

Well, how can anyone be certain of that?

With bare fingers
she dug a shallow grave
placing each one softly down
as if putting a child to sleep
little dead things
covered by moist-cool soil

"be still..." she whispered

as she dropped a daisy
onto the freshly turned earth

it's never easy to say good-bye.

THE GIRL WITH THE BUTTERFLY EYES

~for Cynthia

A little girl
gazes through her bedroom window
and sees an angel, all wings and light

"I know why you are here." She says.

Outside the glass lies a breakable world
bewildering, unknown,
where hope lies closer than fear
and the only thing closer is to imagine…

A young girl peers through plastic panes
of a secondhand dollhouse
creating a world without worry
posable people, static and stiff,
fabricated, yet far more tangible
than the world outside her window.
Inside this miniature,
manufactured menagerie
despair is downsized and detached
this little world,
her refuge and retreat

She learns to swim
by simply deciding she will.
defying the boredom of ropes and drifting
she holds her breath, opens her eyes
and treads the water
                    treads, treads the water.

Seeing the ocean for the first time,
she smiles like eyes do,
rocks jagged, crab-covered,
the hiss of mist and wind

The becoming of words
with new meaning,
a song now soul-deep.
an expression of time
set to salt and sand.

Collecting shells,
each perfectly imperfect
a simple solace and avid attempt
to carry the ocean home

where hope lies closer than fear
and the only thing closer
is to believe…

IN ALL FAIRNESS

~to my Mother, my love for you is a deep well…

My mother always said, "Life isn't fair." This was my mother's method of teaching me to tough things out and she would certainly know better than anyone about life's many grievances.

My mother outlived both her parents, all her siblings, her husband, a son and a daughter. She raised children that weren't hers and never faltered, never once carried resentment, never once revealed fear… I have yet to see my mother shed a tear.

My mother taught me to carry a sense of dignity in one pocket and humility in the other. She taught me compassion and generosity, even when what I have to offer isn't a lot. My mother strongly believed in hand-me-downs, carpools and Sunday school, these were the elements for childhood, resiliency and survival.

In all fairness, my mother was right about most things and she was certainly correct with her words of wisdom…

"Sometimes, life just isn't fair."

Mother swept
the floor of our sorrows
always without shame.

The breached womb,
a breathless child
the porcelain basin where
the downward daughter lay,
our obstinate Ophelia

The stark truths taint cold
the bathroom tile,
the crimson stain
of innocence lost,
the stolen locket of purity
ripped away.

Rosary beads, red and sacred
scatter to the creaking floorboards
and reveal our secrets,
our pain, and our laughter too.

Mother swept
the floor of our pain
always without shame
and somehow always
sees the sunshine
through the rain.

WILD HORSES

~for James Daniel McSweeney 1945-1988

Remembrance is a photograph.
Uncle Jimmy faded to almost sepia,
wearing a top hat in Ireland
behind him, a distant clovered canvas.
I imagined wild horses.
running the hills behind him, free of destination.

Traveling to find answers, something that made sense,
hoping to know more about Grace,
my grandmother, who had been adopted
as a young child. This mystery remains.

October 1988, Los Angeles Sheriff's Department
came pounding on our front door in the middle of the night.
I was eight years old when he transcended to stars.

"Helicopter Explodes Near San Diego"
Who knew bullets would fail to penetrate the Kevlar twice,
or that his feet would never again touch
the bright green hills of Ireland, forever haunting
the stone damp pubs and castles for a surname?

I heard Taps and bagpipes play on that hot summer day.
The heat seemed almost vulgar, prematurely drying our tears
before they hit the ground.

An American flag folded somber,
framed in wooden, triangular repose.

But remembrance is not a flag waving

"God bless America",

remembrance is a photograph. Wild island equine
running the lush, green clovered canvas of Ireland,
a vision tattooed into eternal heart chambers.
I imagined wild horses.

Tribute Paid
llen Deputies

Courtesy of the Los Angele Times (Circa 1988)

LEGACY

Hometown feels like a battlefield
when we lose our heroes.

These brave McSweeney men
took an oath to protect our country
and the freedoms we cling to now
by an ever-fraying thread.

Jimmy stood behind the badge
to protect and serve, and that he did
making history in 1988
when he paid the ultimate price.

William, the Veteran Patriot
and Patriarch of the McSweeney
namesake, protector of our family's
rich cultural history.

Kevin, the Army Veteran
and beloved brother
was dedicated to a better world,
a hopeful place of peace and safety.

And Patrick, a Veteran of Vietnam,
the Cold War and Desert Storm,
he was a talented artist,
a fire fighter, and Renaissance man
admired by all for his
uncompromising bravery.

From Ireland to New York,
Venezuela to Columbia
to the sunny shores
of Southern California
our elders made America their home.

Conflict and uncertainty
stretch from East to West
across this land of the free
but we are not measured by our losses
but rather by our collective gains,
how we live and where we stand.

United by a common truth
that we are more than
our medals and gold emblems
embroidered into life's tapestry

We are a legacy of honor and intention
the guiding light through which
to navigate the dark shadows
of tyranny and oppression.

DESIRE
**This poem is subject to change without notice.*

I want to be certain
I want to be still and calm and feel that I am moving
fast enough

I want to know the landscape of your heart
and nurture the trees there
I want music to sway like ocean and silence soft as mink

I want my feet warm and my dogs content
I want my laundry done, lavender-scented

I want to read poetry to strangers who don't speak English
I want to be lost in Ireland with bad directions

I want to walk through London fog and eat soup
on cobblestone.
I want to share my soup with hungry children

I want my ears to ring like church bells by the sea
I want to eat poems and become them

I want to know the secrets of secrets, what they hold in their
itching palms
I want to fly like Jonathan Livingston Seagull

I want love to taste like jalapeño
I want kindness to be as common as ants on picnic tables

I want spoons to bend beneath my stare
I want things that sing in a sacred palace in an unknown
land to remain undiscovered

I want greener eyes and darker skin
I want grass-stained knees again

I want an endless sunset & sand between my toes
I want chocolate trees and honey wine

I want an end to human trafficking
I want justice for the Epstein victims
I want revenge

I want peace on Earth
I want to finally want something else.

She called me “Armadillo”.

L'ETOILE

~for Leslie Miller

She is the dancer L'Etoile
an Edgar Degas springing to life
brunette hair wound tightly
like Weston's seashell, her toes en pointe
Beethoven's 5th filling the auditorium
as traffic rushes by, indifferent and unaware
Her mother smiles from the audience
holding a fragrant bouquet
of sterling roses, mid-bloom.

Van Gogh's starry night embraces her
each star hanging from her lips
Irises welcome her to this quiet place,
a picturesque Manet boat on a river
she is Venus emerging from an oyster
Her heart painted in pastel watercolor.

Her long awaited "Hello.", shatters Pandora's lock
yet she reaches with choreographed joy
L'Etoile sense of calm brings familiar light
Bright golden sunflowers catching reflections
of a simpler, more forgiving moment in time
that pirouettes on stage of parallel memory
together we are wrapped in silk kimonos
time capsules beneath the Magnolia

*Jusqu'à la prochaine fois mon amie.**

Until next time, my friend...

MARIPOSA

~for Punky

When our hearts cannot find words
and the path to peace
descends long and deep,
may we find our voice
among the hillside's distant blooms

When our eyes run dry of tears
and we are lost
in a haze of uncertainty
may the clouds weep for us
washing us relieved

And when our souls are heavy
with the burden of our grieving,
may hope lift us to our weary feet

When we find ourselves alone
in the weakness of our frailty
may we find a friend full of light
to shed the rendering of our pain

When our brothers mourn
and our sister's faces
are drowned in tears,
may I be that shining sun
upon the hillside's tender petals
in their beautiful, grinning,
gold relief...

And call myself a friend.

all the things i don't remember

The expression in the mirror
this morning reminds of bleak seasons,
a cold February spent sitting
on the door
                    step,
waiting by the mailbox,
listening for the telephone on my birthday.

How could you forget,
our dates 2 days apart?
Was looking at my face
pale and somber
too heavy a reminder
of your failures?

Will I spend the rest of my life
filling the void, trying to replace
the sentiments and loss,
trying to understand,
if you couldn't love me,
how would any other man?

How can I ever love myself?
Am I only the burden of your seed?

I was told I have your eyes,
shall I rip them from the sockets?

I share your same skin tone,
shall I surrender it to the leathersmith
under a cold blade of shame?

Our hair bears the same auburn hue,
shall I singe it at the altar of my regrets?

I have become accustom
to raw disappointment,
to the wrenching of tears under a smile
the disguises you wear, your leaving…

Shall I resolve at a loss,
take to heart your discouragement
and toss aside all hope?

No longer will I send coins spinning
down the well of dream,
no longer shall I be defined by blood
or kindred, nor the coiled helix
that damns me.

No longer will the cycle of destruction
burn my depths to cinders,
branding my skin with
tragedy or statistic,
no longer will my eyes bleed
at the sight of your framed repose

I see your features
in the face of my sisters,
in the mirror,
in memories wrought
with distance and disdain

Your contrition a sunken chest
upon the ocean floor, a shrine of oaths broken,
an endless October skyline by the bay.

But I have since buried the past
in the yard like a lifeless kitten.
Because I don't remember
playing in the mud as a child,
under the old pine tree,
my hands wet with dark clay

I don't remember climbing high
into the plum tree's papery limbs
with strong Santa Ana's
whipping through my hair…

I don’t remember canning jam
with grandma, making quilts
or learning to ride my two-wheeler

I don’t remember the day
I sang on stage at church
in my velvet dress and curls
or bouncing my way to Sunday school
in the old rusty bus.

I don’t remember my graduation, Halloween
or Christmas, or my birthday, or yours

I don’t remember any of it
I was too busy trying to remember,
trying to remember… you.

PATTERN & LIGHT
~for Rebekah

I remember the day, I loved you already…

No one has ever sculpted us
into marble or Medusa

Only a fine *memoryblur*
of pattern and light
dancing off walls
celebrating glorified silhouettes
unaware of beauty beneath the surface

But hope sees something more
a thing of light that moves beyond
spills over oceans
of darkened shadow-cast framework--
barren meadows of misstep

Someone in a field with open eyes
reveals there are dandelions...

Sees vision in *lensblur*
saturation and color-corrected memory
a rough edit, salvation …

fucking forgiveness for once…

In the archway of impeccable light
a refraction reveals itself
an impressionist painting
of what strength wishes to become

A fragrant rose,
sharp black thorns
halo adorned.

WOVEN LIKE THE NIGHT

A Woman told me her story…

she sat on her thr(one)
of secret and uncertainty
as the babe in the basket
drifted away on the tide~
woven like the night

she could have died…

labored breaths, a soft
cry into the darkness - hers.
a leaf rustles in its place
born like tender light

he n(ever) belonged to her…

CHAOS

Somewhere
a bom
          b
is dro
        p
          p
             e
                d

simultaneously

a dragonfly
finds its place
upon petals.

CUT

It began with a rumble
Earth's foundation raging in protest
an earth-angry tremble
deep from the belly of the beast
as we sat still as stone fire
for what seemed like hours.

I imagined the roof caving in upon me
trees uprooting themselves,
running for steady ground.
I imagined flames and angels.

Then, a sublime universal refrain
quieter than the death of a distant star
darker than before the dawn

The sky a sackcloth of blackened tresses
rolled out like a blueprint for destruction.
Suddenly my world resembled a
Hollywood post-apocalyptic backdrop

And I wish for someone, anyone to shout

"Cut!"

FIRE AT THE MIDNIGHT MATINEE

The entire southern California coast
bursts into flame

Radioactive egos tread water
exploding into a sea of cinder

centerfolds and cardboard cut-outs
with their manufactured smiles,
flailing arms, and yoga mats
rush toward a painted
Hollywood horizon
scraping the gum from their heels.

Ushers rip perforated tickets,
viewers take their seats
awaiting the next Black Dahlia

Mouths agape
full of popcorn
and imitation butter.

LIZARDS

~for Sean

Warm California breeze
blows through my hair
I am lucid
the sun a yolk of heat
in the summer sky

I remember you once,
pale blue eyes beside me
in another world, another time
that day we were immortal.

I forgive the past in this moment
yesterday was all risk & prayer
the test of limits in
time-capsule memory.

We were just curious,
key in palm
life was that unopened door…

back then, like lizards
on that hot rock in the sun

we had neither
halo nor horn.

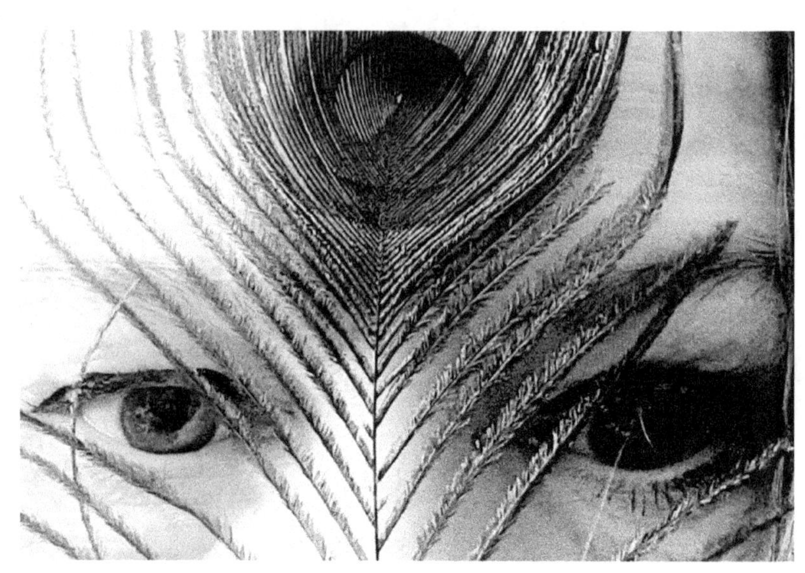

I AM BELLA'S DISCONTENT

Always the awkward feather,
stuck on the chain link fence,
on the collar of a winter coat,
on the windshield,
brushed away as nuisance.

E(strange)d to the world,
comfortable among
broken pottery and hazard signs
lost in the crowd
or wandering that road less traveled.

Small like Alice
in mirrored reflection,
the duckling before the swan
the last one standing--
alone on the edge of eternity.

Always trying too hard
or not enough,
her voice, frail against
the song of youth
the tired truths of experience
quieted, in refrain,
silenced by cold hands
and impatient tongues.

Bella was forever
Mrs. Peacock in the library,
rope-in-hand
hanging on harsh words

Forget me not

GODOT

She wears a sassy hat
a bohemian songstress
with daisies tucked
into the laces
of 16-hole Doc Martin boots

She waits on the brick wall
somewhere between today
and the rest of her life

Waiting for Godot, perhaps?

And I can't help but wonder
why the sad face,
when you look so precious

waiting like that?

VENTURA BOULEVARD VIGNETTES

for Kevin Mattingly & Jenna Wholaver

I.
I apologize for the late-night lament
or is it an early morning mourning?

The news today
live from Ventura Blvd.
announced that Tom Petty
has made a transition,
born into a new era of immortality.

He is essentially
traveling into new womb.
And with this emergence,
a measure of nostalgia
has also died.

II.
Memories flood my senses.
Cruising down Ventura Boulevard
on the back of a Harley.

From Woodland Hills,
to the Hollywood Bowl
and as the stars came out
and Petty took the stage
the music elevated
the spirit of the audience
with Mary Jane's Last Dance..

Tom, you were the storyteller,
the urban legend
the theme song playing in the background
of my anywhere suburbia

III.
Petty meant more than his music
His lyrics immortalized
and brought to life my hometown
and the streets I wandered
singing Free Fallin' down Ventura Blvd.
and the railroad tracks,
tucking into the tunnels
when the train went by
so thrilling!

Petty's songs were
a map of my adolescence,
perspective and good vibes
in a harsh world
where being young
is no excuse and
where curiosity is damned
but wisdom demanded

The magic of Petty
was in his simplicity,
turning 3 chords into
a legacy of heartbreak
freedom and last Dances.

HAIKU

THIRST

Swollen knees buckle
Drinking well distant, deadly
But her children thirst.

TUCSON LANDSCAPE

Mai tai sunset sky
Over desert horizon
Coyote and moon

BE(LONGING)

The moon, a sliced peach
Orion points his arrow
Tucson and my he(art)

LosT Angeles

City to cinders
Buried beneath soot and ash
Paradise wounded

BOUYANT

Sinking tenuous
Deep waters of soul call forth
Plea for buoyancy

MANIFESTATION

Dreamscape revelry
Sacred key in lock opens:
Hidden soul-fire

CONFESSIONS OF A SERIAL

CAFÉ CONFESSIONS #1

I NEED TO BE HONEST
YOU HAVE SAVED ME
MORE THAN ONCE

BROUGHT ME RIGHT BACK
FROM THE BRINK
OF EXHAUSTION
OF BOREDOM
OF ZOMBIE APOCAPLYPSE
FROM THE DEAD EVEN!

YOU SAVED ME FROM
BEING LATE FOR
SCHOOL
WORK
LIFE
EVERYTHING!

YOU ARE THE SPARK THAT
JOLTS ME BACK TO LIFE,
THE NECROMANCER
OF THE CAFFINATED EXPRESS!

CAFÉ CONFESSIONS #2

There we sat sipping Brazilian blends,
among the béarnaise and Beethoven,
marmalade and fresh bagels

The air; crisp as apples
while light rain tickles tin tables
with curious fingers

Umbrellas spread bird-like
against the sky
and we are submerged
as café clatter shatters
quiet cobblestone conversation

We are warm here by the firelight
where Chopin bleeds
through the kiss of rain,
petting the slosh of puddled boots

Hungry hounds
under canopies
await the breaking of sun

We watch beans roast
and floral skirts sway,
Peripherals capture playful spectacles
as a naked toe climbs a covered pant leg

Steam rises ghost-like from your cup
and for once your ocean-blue eyes
seem almost pale beneath the gray

The waitresses
they are all spinning again
and through the cling and clang
of empty cups, I hear you whisper

"One more?"

And my response is always the same…

"I would do anything for you."

A GARDEN OF OBSERVATION

A man and woman are buying flowers
for a familiar landscape

each an intimate landscape
to one another

she wishes she was a rose
and he wasn't a cactus
maintained by her rain

she allows no snakes
in her garden
no trespassers
in need of fertilization

no weeds.

a capella

~for James

I am of the philosophy that a lady must never leave
the room while a gentleman is singing to her.

There is a page I continue to turn to
where a southern pacific marine layer
dissipates over valley horizon

angels are imagined, but fall hard
despite such hopeful wings
there is eye contact over whiskey and wine
a capella rendition of a song few have heard

time releases a universal pause,
music is made, art adored and
poetry perceived in an empty glass
on a lacquered, oak wood bar

he knows the exact shade of her eyes, she his
(she is reminded of clouds)
over the slow flame of Leonard Cohen,
the blue burn of Coltrane and Armstrong

it is a thing of alchemy here in this darkened room,
absorbing the sunshine of each other's bones

DEAR CHARLES,

I wonder if I went back in time
to rewrite history all in rhyme
might we have met in a salacious bar
and made dirty love beneath the stars?

Waking up wrapped in hotel linen,
tasting your tongue still stained with gin.
I ponder how my name might sound
from your lips with words profound.

Would I become a tawdry poem,
your desire, an insatiable, cursed omen,
master, beast, *A Dog From Hell*
seductions of some wicked spell?

Don't leave me yet, I have not said
all I wish to proclaim before bed,
take these words and eat them,
like the fabric beneath my ruffled hem~

YOUR POEM IS A WHORE

I.
She has become cliché
hanging from chandeliers
or sprawled out
on a barroom floor
vomiting on the curb
after midnight.

She's desperate for attention
or direction, a way out
of the dark, a one-way ticket
anywhere, Long Beach
or Las Vegas.

I saw her on a bus bench,
she knows how to whistle
but has never learned to sing.

II.
Your poem is a whore
with a mouth full
of crumbling teeth,
jarring limbs
and a busted jaw.

She spoke the language of
dangling punctuation
and unwanted pregnancies,
used disjointed English,
broken Spanish, and Sailor.

Your poem reeked
of cheap whiskey
and soiled motel linens,
she needed to bathe.

III.
Your poem owes me
money for my wasted time
and my bruised ego.
I am coming to get her.

She was wearing big sunglasses
to hide the black eye.
Clearly, your poem should mind
her own business.

Your poem is a whore,
she's filthy and over-used.
She's told a bunch of lies about you,
cashed out and passed out.

It's not the poem's fault
she is a whore.
You can't blame a poem
for anything.

A CERTAIN UNDERSTANDING BETWEEN LOVERS

Selfish lovers need not apply

Present a tidy landscape

Love can be a momentary thing

Never punctuate intimacy with disclaimers*

Bring the passion

Don’t hold back

Bring the rope

Use your teeth.

*I feel like I should be naming names here.

DRAWING PARALLELS

I visited an animal sanctuary in Belize. There were a number of indigenous animals to behold, and among them was a beautiful spotted jaguar. I watched this exquisite jungle cat as he swatted and flung a wounded iguana around for sport, playing with his food. Years later, I would compare this jaguar encounter to the relationship I experienced with a former lover…

YOU ARE THE CURE FOR LOVE

~ for Kain Alexander

within those dark corridors
where a distant light still illuminates,
and beneath that chiseled stoic visage
is where you cast your spell
like Perseus alive from stone
on a vengeful voyage to spite himself

you cannot tolerate the silence
or the truth it reveals
paralyzing the defenses,
of your unbreakable heart
you lash out at the flickering flame
its warm luminescence
and the cat-like shadows it casts upon
the impenetrable walls you erect
--you tremble at the unspeakable carnage
of its lure and defeat

The burden of my hope reaches once more
through these long shadows
to find an archway of reflection,
through curtained hotel room windows
and dark alleys
the sickness in my heart overwhelms
and i seek that hidden fire,
its heat and glow
a familiar anchor to draw me back
(*because i'll never make it back alone*)
my voice echoes, *follow me.*
follow me back
to where love still has a chance.

CARDIAC ARRESTED DEVELOPMENT, HANDCUFFS AND THIS BALL & CHAIN

give my reality check a ball gag, i need a moment of peace. defibrillation pure shock value, the high cost of living on the down-low has caught me short of breath. as close to death as i am to myself in a mirror, it's all just tired arithmetic. my reflection in the rain puddle is as serious as myocardial infarction; get the paddles. clear the airways, airwaves are playing our favorite song—if only i could hear the lyrics over the echo of my sudden arrhythmia. Thought i died of a shattered heart, but the music just keeps spinning like a broken record in reverse. Let's dance to this blue and red coronary cacophony. i think I just shed some skin.

SPELLBOUND KING CHECKED & QUEEN CALLS MATE

And here we are again
where words are inadequate
and action inappropriate

Both the question and answer render everything
far more fragile than caution should allow
She feels she is a zen garden in a glass castle
carefully positioned, all sacred stones and refrain.

And in another time we might have been lovers
watching a sunset among new green unfolding
in a meadow by the sea, free as fire.

And perhaps, you may have meant every word
you ever said, and I may acquiesce
but instead we sit quietly transfixed,
silent.

LENA BIRD

The day she left us was steel gray melancholy as the yellow mustard crept over the faraway hill. June's weary gloom came too soon. Neither sunlight nor rain would escape that damp cotton prison in the sky. Even the Magnolia with its thick skin held back tears. Weeping for her only on the inside.

IMPRESSIONS OF EXOTIC FRUIT

"And I always dreamed of being awakened with
a caress like this." Anaïs Nin

I.
Little birds sang of you
wrapped in Egyptian linen
as your beautiful eyes close
somewhere in Morocco
where vibrant tiles
and empress dates lie
on a table painted in still-life,
art ready to be devoured

He wishes to paint you
with soft brushes of
light and shadow
draw lines of your landscape
in charcoal smudges.

"I am dying." He says.

And I want to love
every woman within reach

--out of reach--

while there is still time…

Embrace her flaws,
hold silent her scent
captive within dream,
paint her soul
which remains a pale sketch
in a colorless dream

Use blue ink
to capture her words left unsaid
where her story remains
unfinished as bone

*"Love is never simple, it shouldn't be
and I am dying."* He says.

And a woman deserves
to be loved
as I desire to love…
without consequence

Warmed by whiskey
tender rosy peaks
emerge from beneath a silk shawl,
where you are a song
in the hush of taboo
voodoo of womanhood
mistress of madness and passion,
a crimson caress.

II.
*…the future is written upon your palm,
turn over your slender wrist…*

*Poets are born
sharing your peculiar Piscean moon,
they will read your words,
absorb your bravery, Anaïs.*

Words which leave you
hungry, sinful, transfixed
beneath a February moon

We will forever dream
of forbidden green apples,

sublime adornment of
kisses or stones,
love in rich hues of
(scar)let, emerald, indigo
and bask in eternal damnation
for sake of passion,
dress in silk robes
painting our skin
red and unapologetic

We shall sway in starscapes
of your song
belly dance beneath
beautiful moonlit scars

And you will remain immortal,
a sparrow's lyrical sketch.

PANTY-LESS AT THE ANNENBERG ON SATURDAY SEEMED APROPOS

I. *Cassiopeia*

Avant garde in two dimensional
black and white
with a kiss of shiny crimson stilettos
bleeding through a lens
ready to incinerate.
A bicycle chain locked
around cobra-crossed ankles,
fishnet pantyhose stretch thin.
Submission spread across
glossy pages mold girls into women.

II. *Reflections of a Nude Model*

Gazing at almost perfection
is staring down the barrel of
a loaded .38 special

a loaded .38 special
is gazing at almost perfection
wishing to be orchid or child again.

III. *Luminous Transfixion*

She speaks in tongues without uttering
a single word, language is in the eyes,
the anatomical makeup of illusionary grandeur

In her musical movement which
stages the sun as a hot lamp
just long enough to expose luminosity.

Did June ever wonder
who Helmut imagined
when he was inside her?

EN(TRANCE)

Music and moonglow
parade through reticent eyes,
each smile ardently unhindered
by the darkness that steals in
through the cracks of your true intentions

Eyes glimmer with provocation
an invitation to where smoke
curls into corners,
igniting our dreams golden

Amid the lingering
sweet-dry of your snuffed cigar
I am reacquainted
with the delights of you, my Muse
and through your Basil Hayden haze
you declare,

"God is a thief
Your eyes, an endless treasure
of stolen stars."

Your voice ancient like ruby scarabs
daunting as djinn
and when the door to my heart would not open
(artful in your attempts to lure)
you gently forced it ajar
leaving footprints on the clouds
of my trampled dreaming.

SIMPLE GEOMETRY

I often wonder because I do feel that I have been present in these Earthly realms prior to this life, that we all have the otherworldly opportunity to not only experience things past, present & future, but have an obligation to respect the Earth with the knowledge of this...

I thought of the great pyramids
those who built them
touch upon stone
sweat permeating the sand
blistered soles uncountable
of bright stars
ether beyond eyes,
beyond fractured sound or silence
beyond matter...

I thought of great pyramids
against a clear indigo sky,
envious moon
simple pale
imperfect sphere

I pondered ancient scribes
their torches held to light
the bridges they built
with tales of their knowing
grasping in their palm
the only hope of transcending,
scarabs and their legacy,
long journey to the unknown

I remembered silhouettes
against deep endless blue,
a mirage of hazy salvation just—
just beyond reach

I stood there
in another time
tracing the map of my palm
with a quiet finger
closing my eyes
upon a Persian rug
smoking a fragrant pipe
listening to the cobras sing.

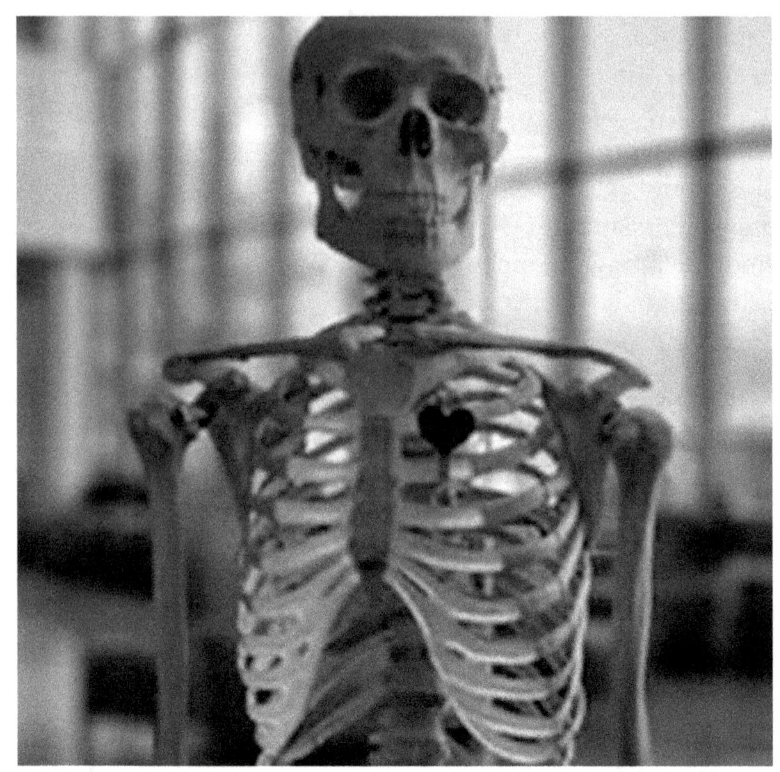

I WAS SMILING WHEN I LEFT THE HOUSE

BONES

I had a dream I was awake.
which makes perfect sense

indeed it is impossible
to shovel bones
when one is asleep.

I shovel bones into
the dustpan of eternity.

No inner monologue
to hush the skeletons
behind my ribcage

skeletons find their
place on the stage
of my heart

and perception
is a mad dance
on a slippery floor.

Daunting,
haunting your
skeletal lies
repeat.

My Betrothed,
disrobe.
Show yourself to me.

THE PEN & THE PEARL

~for Pearl S. Buck

She dreams, she dreams

Silk slippers await her feet
for her to slink away into twilight
upon cold floors,
descending downward
into friendly black hours
when it is quiet,

it is quiet here
in these dark-muse corners
where the moon is her only witness
until dawn paws cat-like
cracking the fragile morning wide open
silence, sage in its slumber.

Ink drips from dry fingers
She is the howl of the voiceless
devouring silence onto parchment
into the psyche, into history
chains of the enslaved loosen their grip
to her words—

she listens and absorbs
the crying wind and walls
walls of oppression and injustice
burst like the sun,

Her wisdom;
a shelter from the storm outside her
outside her frailty, sensibility and belief
beyond a hope she harbors
no demise.

Somehow in this moment,
she is a touch away
a touch away from god
a touch away from truth
closer to the sublime mystery within her
a paradox which curses all she has been taught

no matter

Somehow in this moment there is no time
only movement of hand
the curved landscape of sound
scratching upon flattened white textures,
heavy, stacked like stones

Sea birds soar from shore
and for a moment the ocean roars
in acknowledgment of her finality
in this moment, in this cold, dark corner

hovering above these floor-panels
in her silk slipper silence
the Pearl glimmers immortality.

She lives, she lives…

A DREAM OF EVE'S LAST DAY IN EDEN

she paints herself in mud
to hide her nakedness
and digs a ditch to lie in

wishing to be ravaged
by rabbit or lion

reticent until dusk

do not disturb
the goddess sleeps

her mud now blood

when the beasts do not come
she plucks carrots to lure
from the place
she once planted seeds

they sit on her chest
arms crossed--
only hungry locusts arrive
with sharp tusks

giraffes pattern the fields
where she lay

that is how they found her.

INTERVENTION

i look at you now in story boards, in pictures pixelated, distorted and faded beyond all recognition, and last night in dream i walked beside your grave holding flowers. won't you please wake up? i look at you now in story boards, in pictures pixelated, distorted and faded beyond all recognition, and last night in dream i walked beside your grave holding flowers. won't you please wake up? i look at you now in story boards, in pictures pixelated, distorted and faded beyond all recognition, and last night in dream i walked beside your grave holding flowers. won't you please wake up? i look at you now in story boards, in pictures pixelated, distorted and faded beyond all recognition, and last night in dream i walked beside your grave holding flowers. won't you please wake up? i look at you now in story boards, in pictures pixelated, distorted and faded beyond all recognition, and last night in dream i walked beside your grave holding flowers. won't you please wake up? i look at you now in story boards, in pictures pixelated, distorted and faded beyond all recognition, and last night in dream i walked beside your grave holding flowers. won't you please wake up? i look at you now in story boards, in pictures pixelated, distorted and faded beyond all recognition, and last night in dream i walked beside your grave holding flowers. won't you please wake up? i look at you now in story boards, in pictures pixelated, distorted and faded beyond all recognition, and last night in dream i walked beside your grave holding flowers. won't you please wake up? i look at you now in story boards, in pictures pixelated, distorted and faded beyond all recognition and last night in dream i walked beside your grave holding flowers. won't you please wake up please wake up. wake up. please, please, please wake up! Won't you please wake up!? i look at you now in story boards, in pictures pixelated, distorted and faded beyond all recognition, and last night in dream i walked beside your grave holding flowers. won't you please wake up? Please, please, please wake up! Please wake up!

THAT BOURBON STREET KEYCHAIN

for MJM, wherever you are…

His unique brand of armor was
a certain ambivalence
this was his phantom limb,
an impatient back seat driver,
an unhinged hitch hiker
with a dull blade
and a criminal record.

He was a bold contender of ethics
rooted for the underdog
sober suited him like
an ill-fitting Armani,
itch without rhythm
each day, a challenge
a new war on ego

But today he wanders unlost
through the doors
of a fragmented *Kind of Blue*
with one last turn of key
that profound final spin,
skewing reality like gypsy tea

A gentleman's dark figure
in the doorway is always patient,
standing with hands clasped

a key to your apartment still in the door
with that Bourbon Street keychain
hanging from a vintage brass hook
left to sway upon fixed anchor

you lie there
a perfect storm of silence,

two splintered drumsticks
in your back pocket,
a burned copy of Rain Dogs
clasp loosely in your left hand
while Ken Burn's Jazz documentary
plays on a loop

but ambiance fails to silence
the raw siren of your departure
I collect my things
and lock the door behind me.

DISSONANCE

Show me your carved arrows,
the poison darts of your tongue,
drop your atomic bom
b
s
and I'll remain here
where words are momentary
in this vast space
quiet as death
that lingers here now
a slow-dark silence
filling the glass to brim

Show me your rope fastened tight,
your chalice of hemlock,
your internal inferno.

Reflections in the blood stained
wooden planks, a reminder
heavy as the dead dog
in the hallway.
and the cold ghosts
of failure and demise,
pacing to and fro.

Show me your finger on the trigger,
your hands about my neck,
sharpen your rogue blade and
slay those dragons of
yesterday's curse

THIS QUIET BURN

silence burns
parchment turns to ash
punishment serves no purpose
without redemption

reticence ignites
structures rust beneath torrid winds
elements corrode hollow walls
to wayward distance

silence ablaze
melting ice of another day
washed away, a brackish lake
white noise marks its place
searing hush turns over like tide
as archways burn

trust rusts between the lines
of inaudible destruction

silence burns precious days to ash
banishing a sun's simple ray
treasures lost, wash along
deserted shores

bridges decay beneath our feet
quietude cold,
sheets of relentless snow
and sudden flame.

LADY LIBERTY

Lady Liberty needs to sneeze
In the air, something sinister
And the stoic gaze of the dead-inside
Is the new pandemic.

Lady Liberty yawns,
Stretches her arms
High and wide above the city
She's bored and in an existential crisis
All the NYC pigeons are disturbing her Chi

In refuge from the decimation of war,
From famine and imprisonment
Huddled masses gather in gratitude at her feet
And embroidered on the hem of her robe reads

"GO HOME."

FORGIVENESS ON FLY PAPER

I no longer desire to envision you
Standing on this side of the river.

Stand back with your bloody hands
and your guilty heart

I fold you up origami-like.
plant you as seed.

I bend into my own origami bird-shape,
and fly away as flaming Phoenix.

Grant me my Neanderthal entitlement,
salvation through eye of needle.

My coiled helix requests forgiveness
for these brash imperfections.

I am not ready for eternal damnation.

Not without proper introduction.

FINGERPRINTS AS EVIDENCE FOR THAT WHICH CANNOT BE PROVEN

you remain mystery

somewhere between
sympathy and suffering

bridge above
blackwater and bayou

valley below
bellows of better intention

cracked concrete
before collaps
                    ing

shorn blossom
to save thorn
that riddle in the rose.

MIDNIGHT (MASS)ACRE AT. ST. ANTHONY'S CATHEDRAL

Save the insincere gratitude for the parades and parodies. Take your gratuitous morals and feed them to the circus lions along with my fishbone spine. Have your fog light on when the smog rolls in. How bloody are your hands at midnight mass? I will sit in a back pew, quote the dictionary, chew the cud of religion, sprinkle sea salt on the wounds of your savior. The seven virtues in the stained-glass window stare back. They don't belong here among the damned and destitute. Save the insincerity for the saints. The sinners know better than to trust the wolf wearing a smile.

LESS HU(MAN) THAN HUMAN

You storm our wooden staircase
once a place of tandem journey
no regard for the peace I cultivate
no regard for the love I deserve

Your booming bass interrogates
I am prisoner of your misguided rage
you are judge and executioner
my imperfection a death sentence

I no longer recognize you as human
only this pillar of pointed daggers
that pierce my quietude and sanctity
my existence, no longer justified,
justified resentment marks its place

I fingerpaint sanity on the walls
with my deconstructed gaze
escape into the refuge of shadows
seeking a hidden meaning
behind your piqued and puzzling animus

I look inward and lock away
my vulnerabilities
to sort out when it is safe,
anxiety sways the paralyzed
pendulum of perplexities

I wish for a mirror to
reflect this grotesque figure

who has captured and destroyed
the man of music I once knew

Duality
a two-faced spawn of
crushing realizations
a future haven left to inferno's
volcanic undercurrent
set to smolder in your wake

You have left me no other choice

I
must
abort
mission.

WHAT'S IN THE BOX?

Thanks a lot for opening that locked box
I buried so long ago
that chest I locked up
with as many padlocks and combinations that would fit
then I took plastic wrap and wrapped it completely
like I was Dexter fucking Morgan
On top of that --
duct tape

On the lid in Black Extra Large Sharpie
"THIS BOX DOES NOT EXIST"

after that I took my Glock 19
and shot a full round right into the chest
until it stopped breathing
and I set it on fire
but the box refused to burn
like some impenetrable burden

At last I buried that box
the box with the locks and plastic wrap,
with the duct tape and the ALL CAPS
buried it deep, deep into my past
and there it would remain
quietly forgotten

But you don't play by my rules
you had other plans
you unearthed this box of profound ruin
and now you ask me…

"How are you feeling today?"

A SIMPLE PARADOX

It is easy for a dreamer to dream,
But what if the dreamer is a realist?

Oh, the defining question…

Is the glass half empty, or half full.

If someone has just kindly poured for me a glass of wine,
I would respond the glass is full.

However, be it that I have been drinking
From the glass prior to the question being asked
I would say it is half empty.

It's all about perspective is it not?

DIVISION OF SOUND VS MATTER

While I may not be great at math
I do know the value of a true friend.

Folds of femininity
tease the crux of Cupid's
sordid fairy tale

Mathematics in my mind
are misgiving and unkind

I must recalculate.

THE REALIST HAS A HEADACHE

X. The Mathematician.

X equals a sum of tireless deductions
measured in consecutive losses,

add to this troubling equation
a new level of abstraction
a constant, consolidation
to the simple saltwine of our sorrows

a carbon footprint upon the long
mosaic hallways of this infinite universe.

π The Philosopher

What is one's purpose?
To sustain an erroneous equation,
a prologue to an untimely end?
Or walk alone to carry the burden
of unquantifiable misfortunes
of our own, or of others?
Only to become dust beneath stone
a cenotaph in homage to the forgotten…

To battle with unearthly means, a war
to defend the feeble voice of faith,
only then to fall upon a nameless blade,
or rust as a nail in our own rotting crucifix?

Or are we all a universe
of intricacies upon the backdrop
of one morbid sun
and millions of dying stars,
spinning planets out of reach
existing simply to marvel
in all its opulent wonder?

BLACKBERRIES

Hope is the light you see
a glow beneath the crack of a door
warm and golden
a sacred fire in the distance.

Her lips are the caged bird
which knows nothing but
her howl of savage cacophony

Her eyes are cult of water at midnight
measured in moonglow
surrounded by stones

her hands are a map
charting the celestial cosmos
of your heart

and at sunrise she kneels down
at the edge of the river
risking deep crimson scars
for a fist full of blackberries

DEFINING THE STONE

An old man close to death
holds in his hand, three stones.

The first is a simple river stone,
smooth and gray,
its edges softened by the rolling waters.

The second of quartz and agate
is coarse in texture.

The third stone, jarred loose
from a rugged cliff is jagged and sharp,
yet shiny and translucent in reflected light…

A young boy running on the beach
stops before the old man and the old man speaks…

"My young friend, you have a lot of life to live.
Do you know what that means?"

"I think so." The boy replies.

"It means you must define the stone."
The old man confirms.

He then takes the smooth river stone
and places it in the young boy's hand.
Rolling the first stone in his palm,
the boy observes…

"Each of these stones are unique
and molded by time…
At first, this stone was jagged,
with its edges sharp."

The old man explained, pointing to
the small stone in the boy's hand.

*"A stone's texture can be
softened to smooth by the taming
rush of these waters.*

*It takes time for stones to soften
their edges, but even the largest,
most rugged of stones can be
polished soft."*

The boy held out his hand and the
old man places the second stone in
the boy's palm.

"I see." The boy said.

*"This second stone comes from a jagged cliff
by the sea, but it has been abused by the
crashing of waves.*

*Over time, this stone has become rough
and jagged, but my son, do not be the
fool."*

The old man cracks open the jagged rock
against the smooth texture of the first stone.
When the stone is cracked open
a vibrant crystal center is revealed.

*"The most precious things
are found in the most unexpected of places."*

The old man places aside the
first two stones and picks up the
third stone and continues.

*"This stone is beautiful and
captivating, a little rough on
the edges here and there, but
when you take a closer look...*

"Hold this stone up to the
light, my son."

The boy raises the third stone
to the sun and it shines, casting
a prism onto the sand below
the boy's tan little feet.

*"Do you see? "*The old man asked,
smiling at the young boy.

"Yes, I see.
There is something amazing within all things.
This is a brilliant stone despite its jagged edges."
The boy replied with enlightened eyes.

"Indeed. You must remember, sometimes beauty is not so
obvious. Do you see how this stone illuminates
the world around it?"

The boy then gazed down at the stone in his palm.
When the boy looked up again, the old man was gone
and all that was left were stones on the beach…

NO(THING)

Nothing followed
me into the dark
and already knew my name

Nothing called to me
and I replied

I know who you are

You are like
a familiar stone
or a destination
in a dream
I continue to return to

Nothing followed
me to the edge of the blade
I danced upon the mirror
of its surface

Nothing was there.

I walked to the tip of the blade
I marveled at its beauty
and leapt into the abyss…

Nothing
embraced
me.

LETTER TO SOCRATES

I have not traveled foot spells of brilliant men
Cellini, Galileo, DaVinci
haunted by visions causing a certain madness,
a plight of grander deed or intention

I have not nursed the masses with tender hands
nor fed starving children of thirsty lands,
that was Teresa's benevolent cause;

I know not the algebraic equations
to soar man through ethers
nor how to craft Orion's celestial bow from stars;

I cannot paint heaven's Gods upon
a ceiling's curved arches
nor sculpt beasts of bronze or clay;

Nor can I guide you, torch and tomb
through labyrinths of Purgatory's
red coal & impenetrable iron chains;

I can only tell you this
the hourglass is cracked and we run blind
through crowded streets of our doom;

Time slips through our grip
as we slumber, epiphany's ticking clocks
will further drive us mad;

So dance my fearful friends,
dance fields of dream and wonderment,
rise from your thin sheets and rocking chairs

Sing praises upon infant seeds of spring,
capture death, lock it away in Pandora's ornate box
bury it deep beneath our frolicking feet;

Light twigfire, watch torches and effigies burn
to tomorrow's ash as we stain our lips,
in black wine, devouring the grapes of tenacity;

Swim the chilling ocean currents,
a blue mantra paradise; smile, laugh, make love
and when we are weary from un-hushed revelries

Only then shall we drink our hemlock tea.

AKAMU THE FISHER KING

Akamu the fisher king
whose name knows no age
only the touch of man to earth
tide and bind

He crouches at shore
with line and hook
held as moon against
An Ocean's abandoned sky

All the things
these rough hands have grasp
a lifetime of tribe and testimony
our land to the blade

The fisher king sees life in patterns
the Earth and its dimensions
the land an endless tapestry
of textures and surfaces
uneasy as ocean
and the ocean breathes him in

His hands and feet
are worn with passions
rugged with persistence
(unpossessed by the things he possesses)

Driven only by the tug of line
The carving of canoe
And the draw of Hilo and Huna

HIGHWAY CRUCIFIX CONFETTI

~for those lost on Honoapillani Hwy

This long winding way
weaves through canyon and brush,
strewn seaward with sadness

highway crucifix confetti,
scattered upon
our shattered dreaming…

Last words spoken
last breaths taken
tragedies counted in bones,
souls trapped like caged birds
taken to sky without flight,
lost in wonder, winter
or storm.

~Seven voyeur clouds~

lingering moon-high,
watching from their towers
as souls and hours collide--

Energy and wander
decorate these endless skies
in their vibrant, fractured beauty,
a spectrum of colors mending
in their splendor

And as the whales draw in,
lingering immaculate upon the elements

~they remind us why we breathe~

Their celebratory spouts
spraying forth a somber truth

sung in tridents and exhale,
written in moon and glow

~everything will fall away
everything…will fall.
away.~

Our ancestry, our destinies,
a truth that calls our blood by name
the spirit cathedrals
of our essence forgotten,
like fate lost upon our tired paths,
along this long narrow way,
a weaving lament
of forlorn stones and outcry,
strewn seaward with sadness;

highway crucifix confetti,
scattered upon
our shattered dreaming…

FROM THE MOUTH OF THE MEADOW

~for Monique Hayes

What madness we are
In all our curious spinning…

As Musch Meadow's mouth opens
she has an ancient tale to tell
with the slow burn of sudden sun
awakening the yawning of petals
their colorful morning faces
still sleepy-wet with dew

She speaks of Chumash magic
and the playful frolic of thirsty fawns
still lingering among the tall,
dancing grasses
wandering ocean down,
seaward toward the dry brushes
where we lay down our footprints
the marks of our impressions,
and inspirations.

The rattler coils with anticipation
wickedly ominous as ravens circle
high above the heat of iron and sandstone
he sees the sin beneath the beaded rosary
the nymphs that swim the mossy creek bed
joyful in their smiling mischief
singing of Dead Horse Trail

Among the sycamores
the Humboldt lilies hang like lanterns
from their stem welcoming
the peeking fern unfurling
beneath the man root
that drapes upon the weary oaks

and here we are again gazing ocean down
in all our playful madness
and we are nothing if not grateful~

CENOTAPH OF THE SWALLOWTAIL

... all is unfinished
yet the unfinished is only just beginning...

This is no fairytale,
no Hollywood dream

In the still array of morning quiet
even the birds bow in silence
perched upon tight wires
wings folded in reverence,
their threshold is the sky
for which they need no key

Frankincense burns sweetly
at the altar, no name engraved
they are here to be certain
dressed in dark rain and foreign tongue
smoke spins a web of memory
and gunshot glory

This is no blind plea,
there is no banquet here
no black tie affair

White roses mark tombstones
scattered like black beads
war stories and suicide
decapitation beneath modest stone
blood mistaken for wine
stains her ivory silk

This is no fairytale,
this is where castles
crumble into the sea...
a place of rest for vessels

an abandoned shipyard
of static and still beauty,
chiseled marble visage

A swallowtail nuzzles names
never to unfold like new wings
only memory emerges
from warm chrysalis

Every grave is a cenotaph,
a hushed indigo
epitaph carved in the sky.

LINES IN THE DUST

I am without armor or bruise
in this filtered light
sudden respiratory pause

Upturned flowers mark
the grave of silence
where your songs no longer haunt my dreams

Where did the violet petunias grow?

In the fresh soil where the dead lay
or on summer shoulders
tattooed into memory and scar?

I asked the alchemist to spare my soul for magic
he answered only in raven and black moon,
as silence spirals dawn to dusk
moonlight illuminates the landscape

Never the proper measure for sorrow
the grievance of the accused,
heavy weight of the beholder.

Lines in the dust
and gravity the of shadows.

VANDA

Bleeding cries of death's lullabies
shatter the morning calm
there is no escaping death
or the soft turn of dawn's light
spun to feeble hands and breathless
--still--
among a manic stumble of pleas
dreams turn dark, reality darker
and black suits are coming
red ants marching onward
for this silent vessel, that
no longer reads the palms
seeking answers from the universe
no longer is this (real)m home

Her hands stiff like stones
with eyes fixed upon the gates of heaven
or nowhere at all, I can't be certain,
my faith in these things
is marked by question
broken like pottery,
held like sacrament
against a somber refrain
and the ravens have come
dressed like black Sunday

She is a signature
on a framed certificate,
ether or ash, an amethyst sky
burned into the psyche

CLAIRVOYANT

She is the Death card
held tightly between
index and thumb,
dry flowers growing
soft in stagnant water,
their heads bowed
like funeral shadows
upon vibrant green

she is runes and ancient stones,
heavy darkness laid like cloth
upon wooden slats in the dim
spells spoken, eyes tightly fastened
glowing wax burning in meditation,
elements fused to spirals and alchemy

she is gypsy magic and moonglow,
black prayer and pentagons,
nine lives counted in skulls, four corners
smoke of burning sage,
shell of abalone raised to deaf gods
chanting breath of new blood

she is anointed oil on palms
scarlet linen stretched tight,
petrified rosewood, obsidian
hooves of sacred beasts,
ornate mirrors, morphing reflections,
red wine spilling forth
she is kindling and wet ash
soot clinging to walls like new demons,
paper angels folded in reverence
a cyclops of clarity and vision
movement of shadows in the still
wandering souls of familiars

she is black cats and superstition,
spider and hourglass,
harvest moon, the number 13
swallowing silence, belief,
cauldrons and cawing crows, equinox
and solstice imprisoned in a jar

she is sickles and sewn eyelids
shutters clamoring through silence
blackwater and sacrifice on the bayou
spent matches and sulfur flame,
a sepulcher of bent knees and clasped hands,
veiled mistress of midnight

she is circle, oracle, orb,
painted faces, symbolic sculptures,
congregation of wolf and owl
howling wind and windowpanes,
bloodstains on a Persian rug,
lifelines interpreted, repeated, prophetic

she is clairvoyant.

RUBY CELOSIA

I brush my fingers
through your hair
while you sleep
and plant a kiss
on your forehead

because dynamics here have shifted
you are now the fragile bird
of forgotten flight

but tonight, I am the guardian
the protector of moonbeams
and the forest you call home

I bring to you ruby Celosia

I am the one who wishes
it wasn’t so.

Poet

did the ocean know you would dance constellations so soon?

~for Philomene Long

did the ocean know, Philomene
you would meet Orion so soon,
that you and he
would dance the
cosmos starfire away,
swimming in beds of
constellations and calliope
constructed of ether for you
over venice canals and new moon?

did the ocean know
oh, bohemian rose petal, you
the depth of your haunting
upon steps of these chambers

juxtapose heavy as wet quill
black tourmaline pirouettes
scrawled across parchment?
did the ocean know my adoration
oh, bohemian rose petal, Philomene
decades before

i would read your words
eons before
weight and light of them
upon my sodalite voice
might cause familiar echo to
like a circle of ants climb my spine
eat me whole?
so much leveled to the ground
ferris wheel on the pier
crumbling into silent sea.

such a raven of
cacophony i wish to recite,
oh, bohemian rose petal, you
i shall wait for your reply
in cloud cover and marine layer

toe into water…
ripples
reflection.

PHANTOM LIMB

I. Phantom Limb

It is my own private winter
cold and unrelenting
in this anatomical prison

Where I am less than human
half machine, half lab rat
half alive, half dead
half scared, half curious

Red and blue, pulsating
the mechanical avenues of my anatomy
as lifelines suffocate and confine
an angry itch taunting all self-control

This out of body experience
is out of this world, surreal as
waking dreams and carnival mirrors

This vessel floats on the surface
my phantom limb
has forgotten how to swim

II. Treading water

Wheels spin and sputter
I am on autopilot
destination unknown
Clockwise, and counter
An encounter more alien than human
more voodoo doll than effigy

Bloodlines hold me hostage
Red and blue, pulsating
the mechanical avenues of my anatomy

the blue and red, pulsating avenues
of my anatomy both my weapon and demise.

SALVADOR BLEEDS

"My religion consists of a humble admiration of the illimitable superior spirit who reveals himself in the slight details we are able to perceive with our frail and feeble mind."

~Albert Einstein

The museum is burning down,
the poet's arms are flailing
Ships sailing foreign seas,
fade from dust to ruin

Picasso's lips hold a burning cigar,
while fingers strum his gray guitar

The beauty in the gallery
is not what rests upon the walls
or hangs upon dustless,
soundless halls,

It is not impressions of expressions
trapped in gold leafing
nor figures upon pedestals;
made of marble, carved of stone

Portraits peer back
as statues stare;
eyes visualize,
wondering what we are…

Knowledge like trapped mysteries,
memories of shifted histories
translations of mutations set fossil-deep,
stones we toss river-cross
from our feeble, fragile hands

The ceiling has given way to sky
as rain floods our tears unrecognizable

We exist in time-capsule gray
where we are the modern art
torn-apart on a dance floor,
dripping with blood,
gripping the revolution of evolution

Salvador bleeds crimson into the walls
searching the halls
for the light that Rembrandt stole.

The library is crumbling,
tumbling down,
the poets have all gone mad

Edgar and William grip quills
with clenched fists;
they will not be undone…

And Einstein's corpse is laughing,
dancing with time's uninvited guest

the end…

ROCKET MAN

he has become his own
house of cards
fighting the elements
shooting from the waist
his nervous laughter
collects in glass jars beside
his children's tears
and wishes half granted.

he is the ghost of past selves
the madman pacing circles
in the white noise
he shakes a pocket
full of moonbeams
his connection to the unseen

his long white beard
catches his obscure words
before they plummet
to a lower frequency

he is Rocket man
in a canary yellow race to the finish
he never remembers our names
everyone is a burning effigy
on the barrreling
meteorite of memory

i am my own evil twin
the stoic gatekeeper
of peculiar biographies
and the bringer of light
draping morning across
the thresholds of dawn
i am she who strolls

long after midnight in the ICU
the one who never wins

the ghost in my coffee cup
plays a cruel hand
he is both king and clown
in this waking dream
aristocrats and court jesters
all gather at the dinner table
and the queen has fallen
from her throne

time and space slips
through his bony digits
in slow decay
cognition paper-thin
ready to ignite
complex engines of loss.

his glass jar of laughter
crashes to the floor
as dragons bite
the toes of Rocket man's
jigsaw reality.

PALOMAS ON 6TH

I.
Tucson City Palomas
always flaunting
their gossamer feather boas

Like waif models
skinny gray city chickens
with huge egos
strutting around like peacocks

Head banging
to the sounds of the city
like the whole world
owes them French fries

My bus arrives
and I cant help but think
how envious I am
of wings

II.
Is it that they would rather
scurry than fly?
Have they traded their wings
for convenience and French fries?

For so long you were revered
for your loyal flight
your timely delivery
of letters to mom
professed love pressed to page
words of wisdom or warning
a soldier's last written word

You were the messengers,
couriers of the skies
and the bringers of truth

I watch from the grungy windows
of this tired bus
and it occurs to me
that palomas have no idea
the extent of their wasted freedom
when cooing on the hot pavement
in the middle of downtown Tucson

I watch them through these scratched
windows of bus route 16
and I wish to be somewhere else

I watch them wander
the colorful streets
and I long for
wind and wings.

ORACLE STARLINGS

Starlings in flight
their peculiar formations
mingle with the ghosts
above the cemetery on Oracle Road

a choreographed birdsong,
a dance with the dead
at twilight

here on Oracle road
the sun sinks
beneath the Tucson landscape
into the shadows of ancient Saguaros

where no one is less alive
than the living

GRAVITAS

Grief is a strange and unsettling bedfellow. It is the cold heap to my right, offering no warmth, no promise of comfort. No weather reports. Grief does not tip its hat or draw the curtains, guiding sunshine into the cold corners of my heart.

My grief is a cold breakfast. Always silent. bitter coffee and the bland taste of autopilot on toast. I move eggs around on my plate and count my distractions. I am ambivalent to the house fly praying on the windowsill.

My grief is a carnival mirror, I no longer recognize myself. I brush my teeth methodically and splash water on my face.

My grief is a cold shower. I wish to sleep through this circus of emotion, but resilience pushes me forward and out into the world because complete frailty is a bad look, or so I have been told. At lunch I make chamomile tea as my grief devours my afternoon, each second a new feast.

My grief is a neon sign, I carry it with me to the post office, the farmer's market, the bank and even to those quiet places I go to be closer to the cosmic fire of our infinite universe.

Grief is empty dance floor. And when this grief looms too heavy to bear, it is my overwhelming love locked out of the gates of your presence, unable to find its way back home.

BACKSHADOW

Like infinite stars
she was certain
I rolled from heaven
orchids in my hair

Like infinite stars of divine
pause and refrain
she cried at my feet
begging deliverance

It was I in the
positive 45 degree angle of light,
her, a negative backshadow
in the hollow doorway

Empty of karma, or Jesus or the cross
fingers crossed like promises
In the rearview
an El Paso church massacre.

A curved chrome reflection reveals
a former ghost, a guise,
a phantom rich with vicious vendetta
taste for fresh blood…

Don't look behind you.
Never look back.

LOVE LETTER TO MY SERIAL KILLER

The Glock in my panty drawer
is getting restless
Dita wants to play,

Rearrange your bones on the wall
watch you stumble,
watch you crawl

She has 9 good reasons
and since the doors are all closed
she wants to shoot through dry wall
picture frames and all

Dita wants to smell pennies
She wants to break things
and shatter glass

Dita is getting restless
I think she wants to play
pull back the trigger
cracked bones on display.

MEANS TO AN UNTIMELY END

This glass castle you procured
has collapsed like a house of cards
your perfect façade now remnants
of a would-be American dream

Excuse me while I write this poem you inspired…

You raise your unreasonable expectations,
your voice, and your hand to me.
All the while
embers of your intensity radiate,
the drumbeat bass of your contempt
penetrating the walls of my comfort.

You are no more to me now
than a heavy hand
and a bomb in work boots,
the shark in my bubble bath,
and snake-bite in my shampoo

You and your tired tirade…

Now, with the mask you wear lifted
there is no longer distinction
between man and monster.

NO ONE KNEW HIS NAME

He finds peace in the palm of his hands
fixated on what they might hold
what they once held.

He is the only thing in the city unmoving
As an empty coffee cup
moves down the pavement
propelled by the elements
the visionary smiles
sees beauty in its motion,
it has been given wings.

He wraps himself in the borrowed warmth
of streetlamps casting shadows upon the boulevard
watches rain from beneath the bridge
imagines a flood, no one drowning,
only swimming…

He wanders the city streets
until he no longer recognizes himself
An entire city looks away in vulgar unison
as bells toll from a church a block away,
neon red vacancy signs sear harsh reality
into his eyelids.

No one knew his name.

THE DYNAMICS OF BANANA WARFARE

Based on a true story.

I.
This was a declaration.of war.
Banana warfare.
Conflict began with an unreasonable demand,
a resounding refusal,
and a bundle of otherwise harmless bananas.

The Concho sun beat down on the homestead.
Caveman awakes from an uneasy slumber.
He stumbles to his pipe and smokes his fragrant greens.
Munchies soon ensue, his stomach growls.

Caveman demands ribs.

It's a hard NO for Jane
as she settles into the shade of a juniper.
Caveman, in a threatening manner
grunts and plays with fire.

Jane blinks and drinks from the river.
Caveman stomps mercilessly as profound hanger sets in.
He lights a torch and ignites the juniper
into devastating flame.

Caveman demands ribs.
Jane hands Caveman a bundle of bananas.
Caveman throws them at Jane.
Jane scowls and launches them back at Caveman
hitting him right in the forehead.

Jane makes a peculiar sound and breaks into joyful dance.
Caveman takes bananas in hand and retreats to his cave.

But passive aggressive troglodytes cannot be trusted.

II.
Something rotten this way comes.

Jane awakes to the mysterious yet unmistakable
sweet decay of something sinister.

Caveman basks naked in the morning sun.
Jane shoos a carnival of fruit flies from her face.
With equal parts curiosity and disgust
Jane investigates the haunting sensory overload
of epic proportions lingering in the summer heat.

Caveman grunts loudly and scratches his hind quarters.

Jane remains unamused.

And then to Jane's horror,
located beneath the bushes near her dwelling
were the corpses of 6 rotting bananas,
like 6 long yellow, grenades of civil unrest.
Caveman had used his black magic to curse her once again.
Bananas as a means of emotional warfare…

Jane had learned the hard lesson
that cave men, in true form, were magicians,
powerful alchemists, who possess
the miraculous ability to turn anything
into a chemical weapon.

And so began the Great Banana war of Apache County,
the tragic demise of an otherwise peaceful civilization.

115 DEGREES FAHRENHEIT

I tickle Mexico
to return to you
across desert horizons
of saguaros and mesquite
miles rippled with heat
trundling onto this tired highway,
my bridge back home…

And I could not love you more
as I lean heavy into your indifference,
once my soft place to land
now a shattered citadel
of infinite distances

And those raw truths
that continue to burn and consume
our existence, and each of these
haunting stars above
revealing all our unremarkable postures

How very foolish we are
to think any one of us
worthy of crown.

MANIPULATING THE PENDULUM

We are forgotten until
We relearn the sky and its voice,
The balance of Earth and fire,
The cost of flame

We must remeasure the soil
With our empty cups
And quiet fears
That render us silent
Divide the gold from ore,
Restore the balance of things;
The elements abandoned
As myth

We are forgotten until
We recount the stars
And wheat fields
Which divide us
Sound and distance
From our true purpose
And its bend against
This endless circle
Of survival and sustenance…

But time can be reset,
A universal reversal
As sand vessels fill to brim
And sundial shadows shift,
Centuries of clock hands
Dance their backward spin~
As fossils become diamonds
Under the weight and pressure
Of our sanguine dreaming

And we together
manipulate the pendulum
to rebuild our most
precious commodity…

hope.

ONE HUNDRED THOUSAND POETS FOR CHANGE

APRYL SKIES
BEYOND BAROQUE - VENICE, CALIFORNIA
SEPTEMBER 24, 2011

PREVIOUSLY PUBLISHED MATERIAL:

- A STONE GROWS COLD INN MY GUT - **AmericanPoet.org**
- ALL THE THINGS I DON'T REMEMBER – **PoeticDiversity**
- WILD HORSES – **PoeticDiversity**
- PATTERN & LIGHT – **Edgar Allan Poet Journal #3**
- **LIZARDS – Best of the Net Nominee - 2014 -PoeticDiversity**
- Café Confessions #2 – **Poetry Super Highway**
- A Garden of Observation – **Melaleuca Australia**
- a capella - **Edgar Allan Poet Journal #3**
- Dear Charles – **The Juice Bar**
- Spellbound King & Queen Calls Mate- **Edgar Allan Poet Journal #3**
- Impressions of Exotic Fruit - **The Four-Chambered Heart – In Tribute to Anaïs Nin - Sybaritic Press**
- Panty-less at the Annenberg on Saturday Seemed Apropos – **Cultural Weekly, Matters of Flight and Other Human Tragedies: Alabaster & Mercury, Edgar Allan poet Journal #3**
- Simple Geometry - **Near Kin: A Collection of Words and Art Inspired by Octavia Estelle Butler, Sybaritic Press**
- En(trance) - **Botticelli Literary Magazine Issue #3, Marbella, Marbella, Adelante – Spain**

- The Pen & the Pearl – **In the Company of Women: An anthology of Wit & Wisdom, Sass & Class – Edgar & Lenore's Publishing House**

- A Dream of Eve's Last Day in Eden – **The Juice Bar**

- Thst Bourbon Street Keychain – **AmericanPoet.org**

- Dissonance – **PoeticDiversity**

- This Quiet Burn – **PoeticDiversity**

- Midnight (Mass)acre at St. Anthony's Cathedral – **Rubicon: Words and Art Inspired by Oscar Wilde's De Profundis – Sybaritic Press**

- Letter to Socrates – **Red Fez: Issue #44**

- Akamu the Fisher King **- Hawaii Pacific Review**

- Cenotaph of the Swallowtail – **Red Fez Issue #50**

- Salvador Bleeds - The Ellyn Maybe Tribute Anthology- forthcoming from **Nocturnicorn Books**

- Rocket Man – **AmericanPoet.org**

- Ruby Celosia - **AmericanPoet.org**

- 115 Degrees Fahrenheit - **American Poet.org**

- Backshadow – **Pushcart Nominee 2012 – PoeticDiversity**

- Manipulating the Pendulum – **Marbella, Marbella, Adelante - Spain**

PHOTOTOGRAPHY TABLEAU

ACKNOWLEDGEMENTS

Sincere love and gratitude to my Mother Sheila, my sisters Janet & Cynthia, my Mijas Katie, Rebekah & Rosie Toes Romero, Caitlin And Sam Hawkins, Tim & Niki Simons & (all the kiddos), Robin Smith, Lenny Hutton, Angela & Ricardo Dellarosa, Michelle Molina & Carlos Scalise, Kim Kuntz, Trenelle Lewis, Monique Hayes, Sharon Hope, Kris Kinney, James 'J.R.' Philliips, Greg Bell, Howard Michael & Munki, Hope Alvarado, David Beal, Bill Friday, David McIntire, Neil McCrea, Ellyn Maybe, Pegarty Long, Sean Stephens, Keith Martin, Angel Uriel Perales, Kevin Mattingly, Cklara Moradian, Chuck Powers, Vann Guttierez, & Antonia Alexandra Klimeko.

Additional gratitude to the following people for their continued support of my poetry and for the opportunity to collaborate our artistic ventures: Marie C. Lecrivain, Rick Lupert, Phillip A. Ellis, R.D. Armstrong, Mark Lipman, Alexis Rhone Fancher, Lisa Thayer, Joe Garcia, Richard Modiano, Amelie Frank, Jessica Wilson Cardenas, Billy Burgos, R.D. Armstrong, Larry Kuechlin, Lee Boek, Kalpna Singh-Chitnis, Faiyaj Islam Fahim, Alex S. Johnson, Susan Hayden, Michael Rothenberg, Michael Lee Johnson, Mike Giangreco, Dario Poli, Maria Iliou.

At last, but never least, gratitude to the following angels:
Lisa Crawford, James D. McSweeney, William and Nancy McSweeney, Patrick McSweeney, Kevin Hutton, Danny Baker, Leslie Miller, Yvonne de la Vega, Wyatt Underwood, Steve Goldman, Matthew Joel Marchi, Hank Beukema. And my 4-legged loves Luigi, Lena Bird, Cocobean and Boscoe Bones Jones Capone.

BIOGRAPHY

Apryl Skies is a California native, an award-winning Author, filmmaker, and founder of Edgar & Lenore's Publishing House.

Skies' writing is highly aesthetic, lyrical and provocative.

She now resides among the ancient saguaros, colorful street art and opulent monsoon skies of Tucson AZ.

ROUTE
66

E&L's
publishing
house

www.ingramcontent.com/pod-product-compliance
Lightning Source LLC
LaVergne TN
LVHW010947110826
845149LV00015B/3252

* 9 7 8 0 9 9 8 7 1 1 8 1 2 *